Third Time Luck

Third Time Lucky

Poems by Mick Gowar

Illustrated by Caroline Crossland

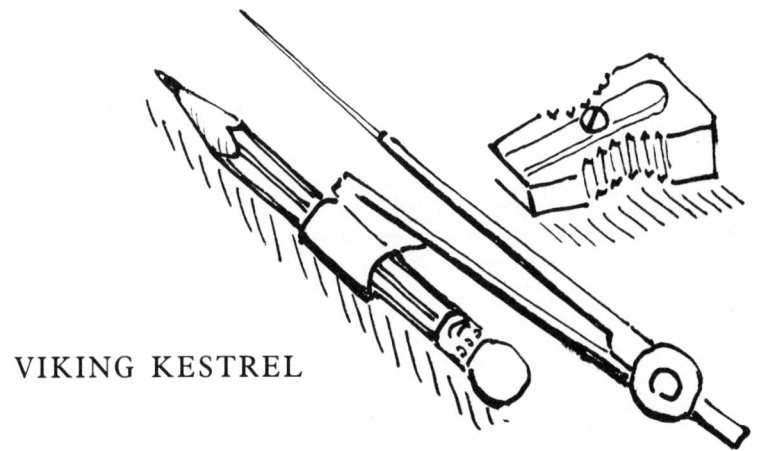

VIKING KESTREL

VIKING KESTREL

Published by the Penguin Group
27 Wrights Lane, London W8 5TZ, England
Viking Penguin Inc., 40 West 23rd Street, New York, New York 10010, USA
Penguin Books Australia Ltd, Ringwood, Victoria, Australia
Penguin Books Canada Ltd, 2801 John Street, Markham, Ontario, Canada L3R 1B4
Penguin Books (NZ) Ltd, 182–190 Wairau Road, Auckland 10, New Zealand

Penguin Books Ltd, Registered Offices: Harmondsworth, Middlesex, England

First published 1988

Text copyright © Mick Gowar, 1988
Illustrations copyright © Caroline Crossland, 1988

All rights reserved. Without limiting the rights under copyright reserved
above, no part of this publication may be reproduced, stored
in or introduced into a retrieval system, or transmitted, in any form
or by any means (electronic, mechanical, photocopying,
recording or otherwise), without the prior written permission of both
the copyright owner and the above publisher of this book.

Printed in Great Britain by
Butler and Tanner Ltd, Frome and London
Filmset in Linotron Plantin 12/14pt by
Rowland Phototypesetting Ltd, Bury St Edmunds, Suffolk

British Library Cataloguing in Publication Data
Gowar, Mick, *1951*–
  Third time lucky.
  I. Title
  821'.914

ISBN 0–670–81492–X

Contents

Fruit	7
Love Poem	8
Sisters	10
Mirror Games	14
Machine Riddle 1	16
Cholmondeley	18
Annabell and the Witches	20
Watch It or Else	28
Machine Riddle 2	30
Mum Takes a Bath	32
Hunting with Henry the Cat	34
Season's Greetings	38
Living Doll	40
Machine Riddle 3	44
Junior School Sports	46
Barry	50
Hide and Seek	53
New Leaf	56
Machine Riddle 4	58
Dentist's Lament	60
Best Friends	63

Day Dreaming	64
Building a Snowman	66
Scary Monsters	68
Shoplifting	71
Boots	73
Index of First Lines	76
Answers to the Riddles	77

Fruit

Some things are true
And some are only true in school.

Like fruit. We did fruit
Today in Science. We learnt

A tomato's a fruit but
A strawberry isn't.

I copied down the diagrams
And all the notes

'Cos I knew I had to
Pretend it was true.

I'm not daft, I know when
To make-believe:

That's why I'm
Set One for Science.

Love Poem

If I can get from here to the pillar box

If I can get from here to the lamp-post

If I can get from here to the front gate
    before a car comes round the corner . . .

Carolyn Murray will come to tea

Carolyn Murray will love me too

Carolyn Murray will marry me

But only if I get from here to there
    before a car comes round the corner . . .

Sisters

Sally hasn't talked to me for ages.
    She shouts, she swears
    She sneers and jeers, she rages
    She stamps around and slams the door
But doesn't *talk*.
All she'll say to me these days is
'Get lost, go away,
Leave me *alone*!'

Sally hasn't laughed with me for ages.
    She doesn't smile
    Or grin or giggle,
    Won't share a joke.
And when I tell her something funny
She throws her eyes up to the ceiling
Says, as if to someone else:
'Why don't that stupid kid shut up!'

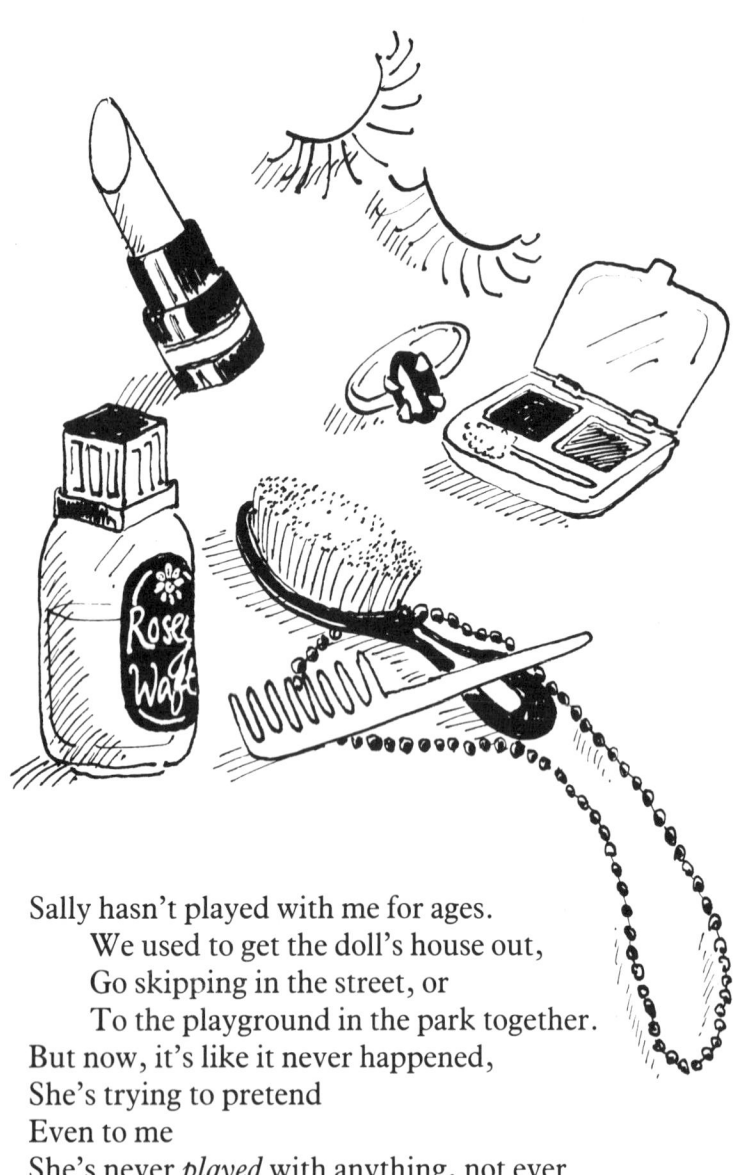

Sally hasn't played with me for ages.
>   We used to get the doll's house out,
>   Go skipping in the street, or
>   To the playground in the park together.
But now, it's like it never happened,
She's trying to pretend
Even to me
She's never *played* with anything, not ever.

Sally hasn't wanted me for ages.
> She's getting too *grown-up*
> To be seen with me,
> She reckons.
But I can get my own back, don't you worry.
It's nearly bedtime and I've hidden
The teddy bear
She sleeps with every night.

(And in a little while we'll see
How grown-up my sister Sally
Really is . . .)

Mirror Games

If you come round to play with me
In my back garden,
And after tea
I say:
>'We'll play
>Robin Hood.
>You can be the wicked Sheriff
>Or his Captain
>(I don't mind – you choose).
>I'm Robin.
>You've got me locked in prison
>But we have a big fight
>You lose!
>Then I tie you up
>To the apple tree
>And gallop away free!'

Then that's what we should do.
It's only fair –
We're in *my* garden
And I always have the best ideas.

But if you say:
>'I'm the guest so
>*I* should win.
>I'll be Robin
>And you're the baddy –
>*This* is what happens:
>You've got me tied up,
>You're going to torture me
>But I'm too strong –

I break free!
Then I bash you on the head,
And stab you through the heart
And then you're dead!'

Then you're just being bossy,
Throwing your weight around
Again.
You're such a – *Big Head*!

Machine Riddle 1

What can kill a man
– quick as a flash –
is life's blood to me.

I'm the great eater,
the magnificent cruncher!
Feed me! Feed me!

I'll eat all your rubbish,
your greatest treasure;
I'll eat all your jobs,

then I'll eat your leisure.
Any old bones, any old logs,
it's all the same to me.

I'm the mad cuckoo,
pack my craw.
'More,' I scream – 'MORE!'

You are my servants,
my keepers, my feeders,
stunned by the speed I digest.

And I am the cuckoo,
the mad, mad cuckoo
– and the whole world is my nest . . .

(Answer on p77)

Cholmondeley ★

A cholmond of mine
Named Cholmondeley
Was stung one afternoon
Most horribly
By a bolmondble bee

(Or it might have been a holmondble bee,
Cholmondeley didn't see).

Cholmondeley was pottering happily
In his garden, when he noticed
– 'Burp! Pardon me!' –
His tolmondy was getting rolmondbly.

He thought, 'I'll pick
A ripe, juicy plolmond
From my plolmond tree.
That should do the trick . . .'

When suddenly –
'Aieeeeeeeeee!'
That dreadful bolmondble bee
(One of the vicious sort)
Flew up the leg of Cholmondeley's shorts

And stung him
On both cheeks of his bolmond!

Poor Cholmondeley –
What agony!
He grabbed his bolmond and
Dropped his plolmond.

A double tragedy:
Poor Cholmondeley lost his plolmond,
And all he got in return was
A nolmond bolmond!

*Cholmondeley is pronounced 'chumly'.

Annabell and the Witches

Once upon a time there was a girl called Annabell.
Her mother said she was –
   a sweet little girl
   a dear little girl
   a nice little girl.
But Annabell didn't like that one little bit,
because Annabell wanted to be
A WITCH!

Not any old kind of witch –
no, Annabell wanted to be
   a nasty witch
   an ugly witch
   a nasty, ugly, evil witch . . .

WITCH
N., U. & E. Ltd.

The only trouble was
Annabell didn't know any witches,
so she was having a hard time
learning how to be nasty, ugly and evil.

Until, one day, she had a brilliant idea:
She looked up 'Witch' in the phone book!
And she found:
WITCH, N., U. & E. Ltd, On the Common. And
   then a phone number: Nasty Weather 1200.
But when she rang the number
all she got was
a nasty, ugly, evil slurping noise –
the witches' phone had been
                        Cut Off!
So Annabell wrote the address
on the back of her hand,
waited until the weather was *really* nasty
and went to the Common
                        All Alone . . . !

When she got there, she saw
three witches dancing round a big black pot.
They were singing:
>'Hubble, bubble, boils and spots,
>Gravy full of slimy clots,
>Smelly socks and filthy rags
>And things that live in dustbin bags . . .'

'That sounds *great*!'
Shouted Annabell. 'Let me have a go –
I want to be a witch, too!'

The nastiest, ugliest,
most evil-looking witch spun round.
She glared at Annabell.
Then she asked a nasty question:
'Can you spell?'
'Yes,' said Annabell,
'. . . a bit.'

'You can't be a witch without a spell,'
sang all the witches together.
'And you can't make a spell until you can
S-P-E-L-L!'
'I'll show you,' said
the nastiest, ugliest,
most evil witch.
And she began to sing
in a voice so scratched and tuneless
that it made Annabell's teeth cringe:

'*S*low and slimy, cold and clammy
*L*ike a lump of
*U*ncooked liver.
*G*reen revolting slithering slug.
Slug with silver slime trail oozing,
S-L-U-G I spell and
                     Slug you be!'

And Annabell felt her body shrink
– smaller and smaller
and her skin become cold and wet.
And suddenly
all she could see
stretching high above her
were stalks of grass
– as tall and thick as apple trees.
And the tiny grains of soil
felt like great rocks
beneath her one wet foot.
And all she could hear was the
'Arkh, Arkh, Arkh!' cackle
of the witches laughing at her.

Then the ugliest, nastiest,
most evil witch stopped laughing.
She cleared her throat
and began to sing another song:

'*P*orker
*I*n the pigsty
*G*runting –

Swell my swill-pig fat with lard.
Balloon of bacon, pink and pudgy –
P-I-G I spell and
                     Pig you be!'

And as the witch sang the last line
of the spell,
Annabell turned back from a slug
into a girl . . .
                but only for a moment.
Annabell felt herself swell.
And the pretty pink bow
her mother had tied
at the back of her dress became
a pink curly tail.

And the pretty pink bow
her mother had tied
in her hair turned into   Horkh!
two, huge flapping ears.   Horkh!

'Stop it!' she shouted.
'It's horrible!'
But the only sound
that came out
of her little piggy snout was
'Horkh! Horkh! Horkh!'

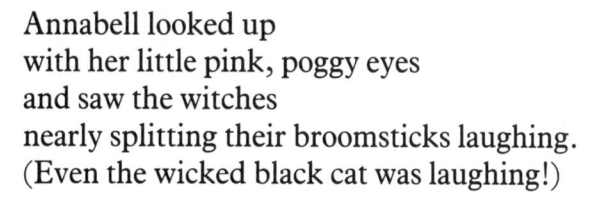

Annabell looked up
with her little pink, poggy eyes
and saw the witches
nearly splitting their broomsticks laughing.
(Even the wicked black cat was laughing!)

Then the nastiest, ugliest,
most evil witch
wiped the tears from her eyes
with the filthiest handkerchief
that Annabell had ever seen
and sang:

'*A*s you were –
*N*ot grunting pig
*N*or slithering slug but
*A*s
*B*efore.
*E*verything be
*L*ike it was, and
*L*et you be
        A-N-N-A-B-E-L-L once more.'

And Annabell was back on the Common.
As a girl.
Alone!
The witches had . . . Vanished!
(But she could still hear
a nasty, ugly,
evil laugh
echoing, echoing away in the darkness . . .)

There was nothing left,
so Annabell started to walk home.
But as she walked she sang:

'*S*lug was nasty, slimy, horrid.
*P*ig I never wanted to be.
*E*veryone, please
*L*eave me alone! Just
*L*et me be Annabell . . .
                  Let me be M E!'

Which wasn't bad
  for a beginner . . .
                  Was it?

Watch It or Else

Some kids have fairies or friends you can't see
   Who live in their garage or garden,
And they do soppy things like invite them to tea –
   But I've got a couple of hard men!

I've got a pair of invisible minders
   (Like Tough Guys you read of in Thrillers),
Called Vicious and Mean-man, they're both eight feet tall
   And as strong as a pair of gorillas!

Deep in the nettle-patch down by our shed
   They hide from the light through the day.
But when night starts to fall, I can send them both out
   To bash up whoever I say!

So you'd better stop picking on me, *Darren Bates*,
   And you'd better believe me – it's true!
I've told them about you. Tomorrow – you wait!
   They'll be here, by the gate . . . just like you!

Machine Riddle 2

I am the breaker of bones
I am the fouler of air
   Watch out for me once
   then twice
   then again . . .
Beware, oh beware!

I am the beast of sight
I can find my prey anywhere
   I can see what's to come
   what is now
   what is past . . .
Beware, oh beware!

And at night by my beacon sight
I follow a trail to my lair
   The gleaming spoor of
     blood-
       red
         eyes . . .
Beware, oh beware!

(Answer on p77)

Mum Takes a Bath

On a normal, average day in our house:

Tracey and Darren
   are fighting with Sharon,
the TV set's blaring,
   and Gran's started swearing,
the cat caught his paw
   when Michelle slammed the door
and he's rowling and yowling in pain;
once again, baby Shane's
   stuck his hand down the drain
and he can't get his thumb out
   so he's screaming his lungs out:
the shrill accusations
   and reverberations
of the whole pandemonium's mass aggravations
   are shaking the house from the roof to
     foundations –

I go to the bathroom
   and lock myself in.

I go to the bathroom
   and shut out the din.

I go to the bathroom and turn on the taps.
   And I peel them all off like a skin.

Because
   in the water
     the warm, silky water
       the deep, soothing water
with my ears under water
I can't
     hear
         a thing . . .

Hunting with Henry the Cat

Small black-and-white cat –
white face, white tummy, white paws
sharp eyes, sharp ears, and
. . . very sharp claws

stretches out along the floor
scratches round his bowl, then

out of the door to the garden.

(But don't be fooled by his
slow and sleepy, easy walk – he's going
                        hunting!)

A sunny path,
              he's lying with his front feet in
                                      the air.

(He's very, very still,
he's *not* asleep . . .)

    SNAP!

He's missed . . . a butterfly

Two wings of creamy-white
like fluttering crisps

(A snack that got away –
to flutter back another day?)

Rolls over, up and
prowling now – a Tiger in a Forest of
Chrysanthemums . . .

He's *hunting* – yes, but *what*?
          Caterpillars? . . . Centipedes?

(Anything That Moves, says Henry.)

No luck,
        the sun's behind a cloud, so
back indoors he comes
but hunting isn't finished
just because he's in the house –

Not while we've got that sling-back chair
and Henry's rubber mouse!

Drop the mouse in,
   ripple the seat from underneath

Henry leaps and grabs and twists –
rolls right down on to the floor
for a game of
          Push and . . . Pounce!

Or dribble the mouse around the carpet
   on the tips of needle claws.

(But don't forget,
through Henry's eyes it's
only half a game
          or even less.)

Teatime comes
I open up his tin –

Henry's there already,
he heard the cupboard door and
jumped up through the serving hatch.

He's rubbing round my ankles
   underneath my feet
             nearly tripped me up . . . 'Stop it!'

I put his bowl down.
'Eat it all up.'

(I don't need telling, Henry says.
I haven't caught a thing *all day* – I'm *starving*!)

Season's Greetings

In Art we're always drawing cards
For Hallowe'en or Easter,
Christmas, Harvest Festival,
Each holiday or feast or

Mother's Day or Father's Day,
Any old excuse is
Time to draw *another* card.
I *hate* it – 'cos I'm useless!

I couldn't draw the Easter chicks
   I couldn't draw their eggs,
I couldn't draw the bunny's ears
   I couldn't draw his legs.

I couldn't draw a harvest sheaf
   I couldn't draw a plough.
I couldn't draw *then* and
   I can't draw now!

Look!

I can't draw robins
   I can't draw snow,
I can't draw holly
   I can't *draw* – no!

I can't draw turkeys
   I can't draw stuffing,
I can't draw Santa Claus
   – I can't draw nuffing!

So *please*, Mrs Stevenson,
Give it a rest!
Don't say, 'It's very nice, and
I can see you've done your best.'

I couldn't give it to my Granny,
Or even to my Aunt –
'Cos I can see it's terrible
Even if *you* can't!

Living Doll

My sister was only
nine years old
when love first struck her
like a thunderbolt!
Six weeks before Christmas
she fell in love
with a *doll*!
A special doll that
(so the adverts claimed)
'has hair that *really* grows!'

One flick of the tiny
plastic switch and
– '*so* easy' –
the neat blonde crop was
suddenly a pony tail.
Another flick and
– 'in an instant' –
a waist-length mane
of golden curls.

She wrote to Father Christmas:
'Please, oh please,
Please – PLEASE!'

She didn't get one.
She got a bike instead
(bought weeks before
and hidden
in the next-door neighbours' shed).
She sulked all Christmas.

My Mum and Dad were sure:
'She'll grow out of it by June'
(her birthday).
They were wrong.
This wasn't 'just *another* craze'.

She kept it up
from January to June –
five months of hints
and pleading. Then,
as time grew short,
begging letters.
Finally, she left
imploring messages
on the Ansaphone.

They gave in –
bought her one,
of course.

Her birthday morning.
She tears downstairs,
heart pounding in her throat,
scattering the pile of parcels
on the breakfast table.
There *must* be one.
Is this . . . ?
She skins it – yes!
It is!

A scream of delight and
she runs upstairs
into the bathroom
and locks the door.

Silence.

We sit at breakfast
staring at the untouched presents.

The silence grows,
becomes
suspicious,
unnatural,

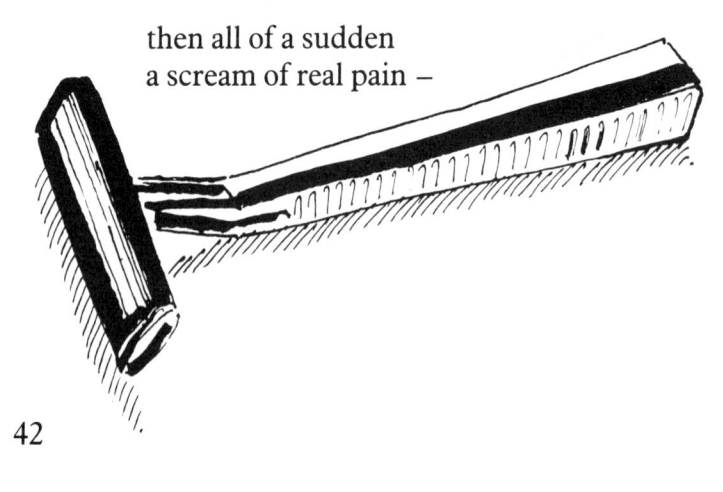

then all of a sudden
a scream of real pain –

we leap the stairs
three at a time . . .
and there
in the bathroom,
tears streaming down her cheeks,
my sister stands:
the doll in one hand,
my father's razor
in the other.

'Grow!' she pleads.
'Please, *please* grow!'

The bald doll grins
its plastic smile,
unmoved.
All around my sister's feet
the dreams,
the lovely dreams –
the thick, rich, golden curls
lie. Hacked into

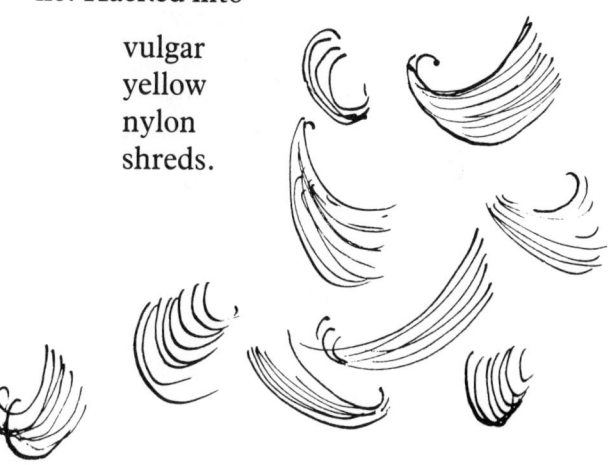

>vulgar
>yellow
>nylon
>shreds.

Machine Riddle 3

My father was the mirror on the wall
(You know the one, I'm sure you've heard the tale):
Informed on Snow White, bugged the Seven Dwarves
And drove the queen from vanity to murder!

My mother was a hag, the Wicked Witch
Dreaded at all the Royal christenings.
The spindle trick was Mum's idea of fun
– A great one for the magic boomerangs!

So I was brought up in the family trade
Of alchemy and magic, charms and spells.
But came the time for me to make my mark,
No one believed in all that any more.

The next two hundred years were really tough.
We scratched a living reading sweaty palms
In fairgrounds, curing ague, laming horses,
Performing conjuring tricks in music halls.

Then Mum and Dad retired. I saw my chance.
I brought the family business up to date:
Instead of amulets and crystal balls
– The Magic Lantern and the Phonograph!

(Answer on p77)

Since then I haven't missed a trick – see here:
Lasers, chips and integrated circuits,
Satellites . . . But look a little closer,
The game's the same, just as it always was.

Still granting wishes, casting spells and curses;
Still spinning straw to gold (and vice versa).
But *now* one spark, one newsflash or one ad,
And – snap! – the whole world's in my service!

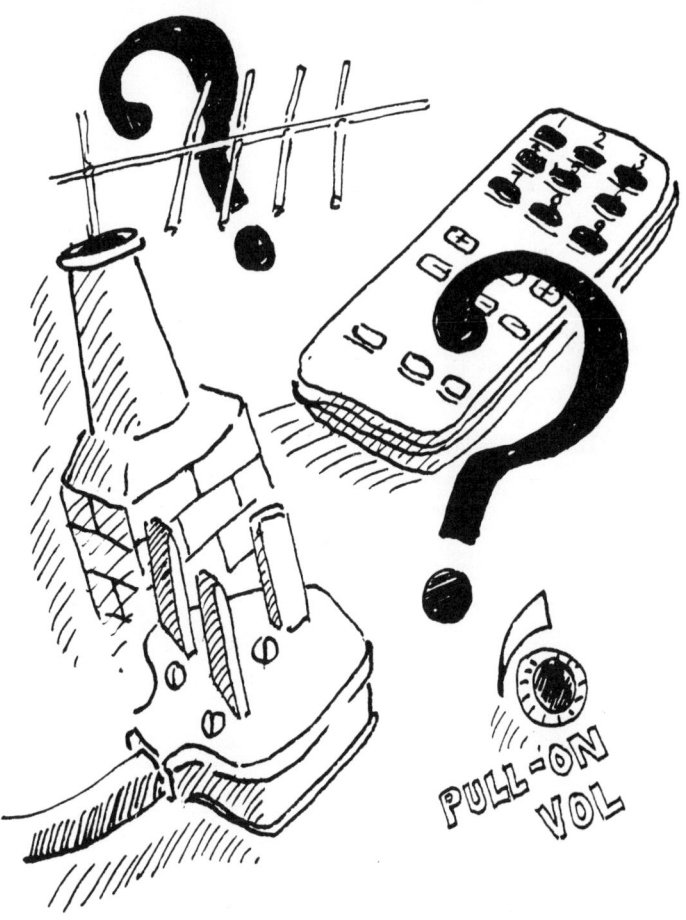

Junior School Sports

Sports Day's over.
It's four o'clock.
The mats have all been stacked away,
the benches and the chairs
all cleared away,
the Mums and Dads and little kids
have all gone home for tea.

There's just a handful of us
Fourth Years stayed behind
to help collect up all the bean-bags,
hoops and balls
and batons from the relay.

Sports Day's over.
But what a great day!
I won the rounders ball,
a throw of 40 metres – beat the record!
The one thing, maybe the only thing,
I'm *really* good at.
This has been the best day of my life.

The last week
of the last term
of the Fourth Year.
Tomorrow is the very last day

*and I don't want today to end
I want to stretch this afternoon out
like a rubber band, I want
this afternoon to last
for ever.*

Daft!
I know it can't.
I've seen all year how
everything's too small,
how I've outgrown it all –

the chairs too low,
the corridors too narrow,
the climbing ropes too easy,
the playground and the hall too cramped

Sports Day's over
and that's that.
At my feet
the last wire crate of rounders balls,
the last thing
waiting to be put away.

Next year
It'll all be different.
I'll be a First Year then,
just **a little kid** again.
I won't be best at anything next year!

Go on, girl –
one last throw?

A short run –
                back foot
              front foot – **Hurl!**

Watch it soar –
20 – 30 – 40 metres . . . Go on! Go on!
50 – 60 . . . Don't stop! Don't ever stop!
See the white ball
arc across the clear blue sky –

'**Julie!** I'm surprised at you!
This isn't the time to
mess about.
Go and get it
   – **now!**'

'Yes, Miss. Sorry, Miss.
Don't worry, Miss,
It won't happen again –'

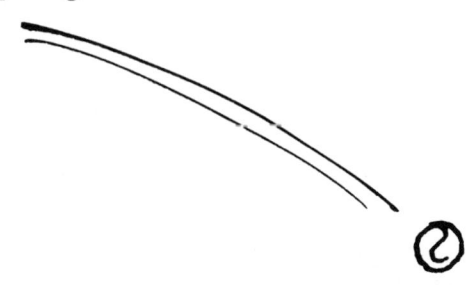

Barry

The teachers saw
a big, round, open, honest face.
A laughing, happy, jolly boy.
They noticed he was clumsy,
but good-natured
and always ready to help.

So popular.
Just one look was enough
for an *experienced* eye
to be completely taken in.
Barry was an artist
in the craft of bullying.

'Oh, Miss, I *am* sorry.
I tripped and spilt my water
all over Michael's painting
and he'd been working
so hard on it
for Parents' Evening.'

To me (but for her benefit):
'I'll help you
clear it up.
I am *so* sorry.'
The painting, not quite ruined,
is swiftly obliterated by

his eager attempts
with paper towels
to make amends.

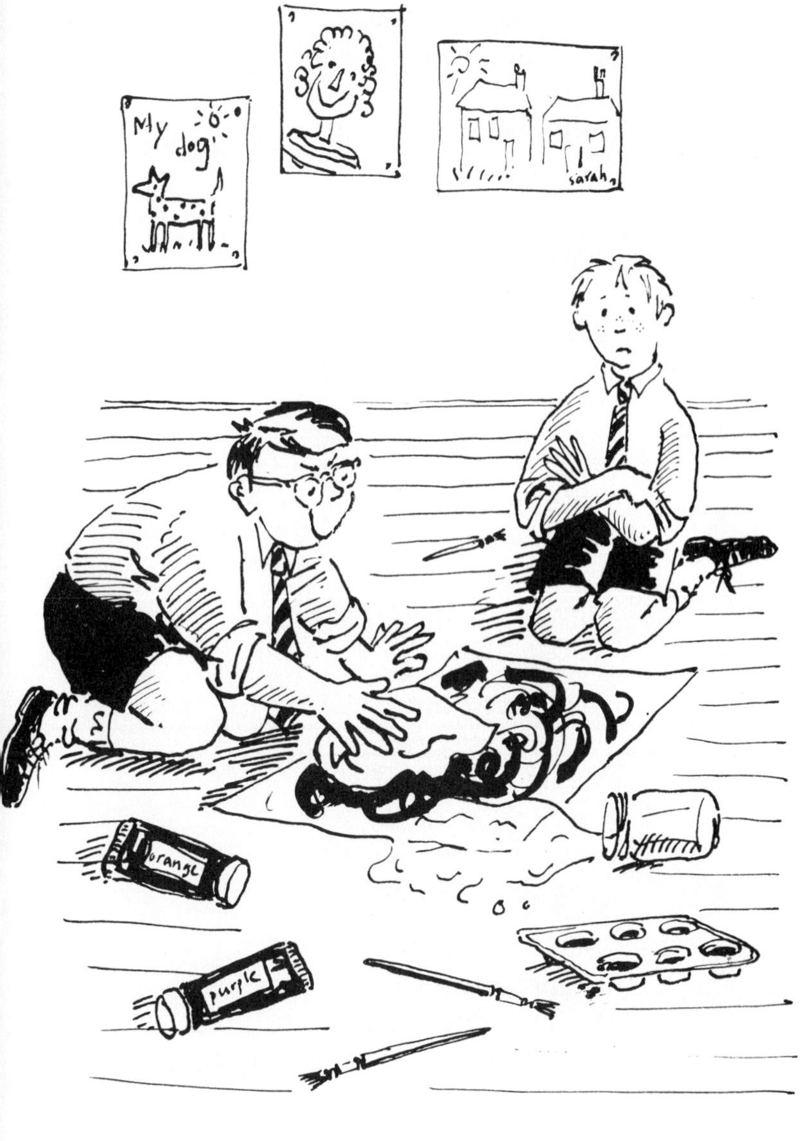
My dog
sarah
orange
purple

In the playground, after Art,
the broad grin and
the hand clamped on the shoulder
say to the whole world
(any teachers watching?)
We're good mates:

no – *Best Friends*.
No one that matters ever hears
(as fingers grip and twist
the pinchful of flesh
on the neck, behind the ear)
the yelp

covered by him
bawling out a joke
at the top of his voice.
Only the ice-bright glint
behind the eyes is real,
the needle stare:

'You forgot my
little present
this morning.
I waited by the gate,
but you were late.
You're getting careless.

Accidents happen to
people who break their promises.
So don't forget tomorrow
                    – right?'

Hide and Seek

Hiding here
   on the floor of the shed
dark as a rabbit hole
   under the bench
the sharp tang of creosote
   itching my throat
and splinters like fingernails
   snagging my hair

'You'll never find me
   You'll never find me'

Hiding here
   on the floor of the shed
in the gloom and the darkness
   under the bench
where no one has been
   for years and years
in the darkest shadows
   the sun never reaches

'You'll never find me
   You'll never find me'

Here in the dark
   in the damp and the dust
in the sawdust and shavings
   the dirt and the muck
where spiders and woodlice
   can crawl up your legs
and worms and all slimy things . . .

   'I'm coming out.
*See – **you** never found me!*
   You never found me . . .'

New Leaf

Today is the first day of my new book.
I've written the date
and underlined it
in red felt-tip
with a ruler.
I'm going to be different
with this book.

With this book
I'm going to be good.
With this book
I'm always going to do the date like that
dead neat
with a ruler
just like Christine Robinson.

With this book
I'll be as clever as Graham Holden,
get all my sums right, be as
neat as Mark Veitch;
I'll keep my pens and pencils
in a pencil case
and never have to borrow again.

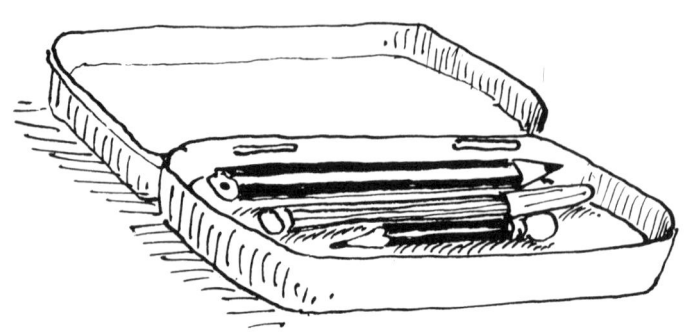

With this book
I'm going to work hard,
not talk, be different –
with this book,
not yell out, mess about,
be silly –
with this book.

With this book
I'll be grown-up, sensible,
and every one will want me;
I'll be picked out first
like Iain Cartwright:
no one will ever laugh at me again.
Everything will be
different

with this book . . .

Machine Riddle 4

I started as an empty tortoise shell,
The stretched and twisted sinews of a goat.
I wasn't meant to be what I became . . .

I was an accident, an abacus
That failed. Invented by the Greatest Mind
In All the World: his butter-fingers dropped
The beads – how typical! So what was left?
He didn't know; and so he gave me to
His idiot child. The gangling boy clawed
At my sinew strings –
    The sound was awful!

Over the centuries my neck grew long,
My inlaid wooden belly full and round.
My tongue grew sweeter than the nightingale's –
So I became the voice of *love's young dream*!
Under a thousand windows, a thousand
Spotty youths would shriek and pluck in honour
Of their ladies fair –
    The noise was ghastly!

Now: I am an axe, a howling chainsaw,
A shrieking weapon of the young berserk
Hell-bent on wealth beyond their wildest dreams!
And by each note, each chord, they calculate
Another thousand bucks is in the bank!
So in a way I'm back where I began . . .
And the sound is ghastly, awful –
    Worse than ever!

(Answer on p77)

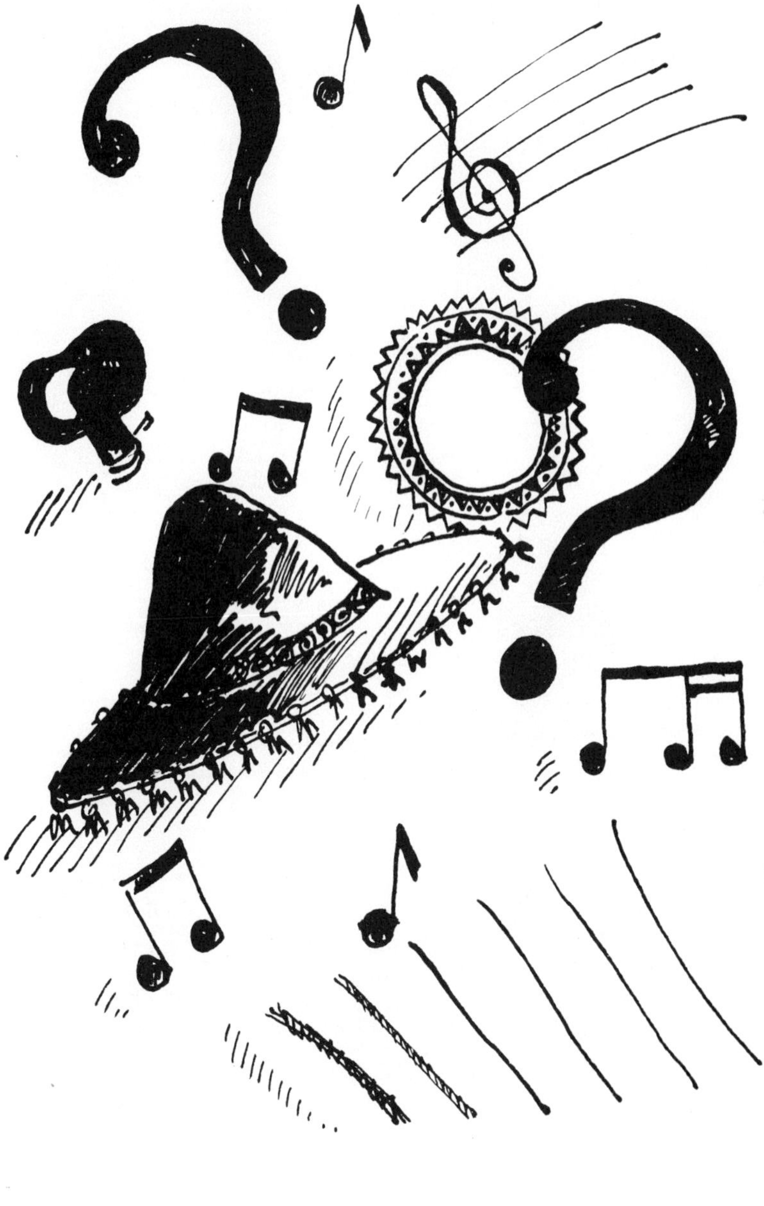

Dentist's Lament

I give them 'Natural Nashers' badges,
Stickers saying: 'Let's Beat Plaque
– Together!',
Tell jokes and riddles.

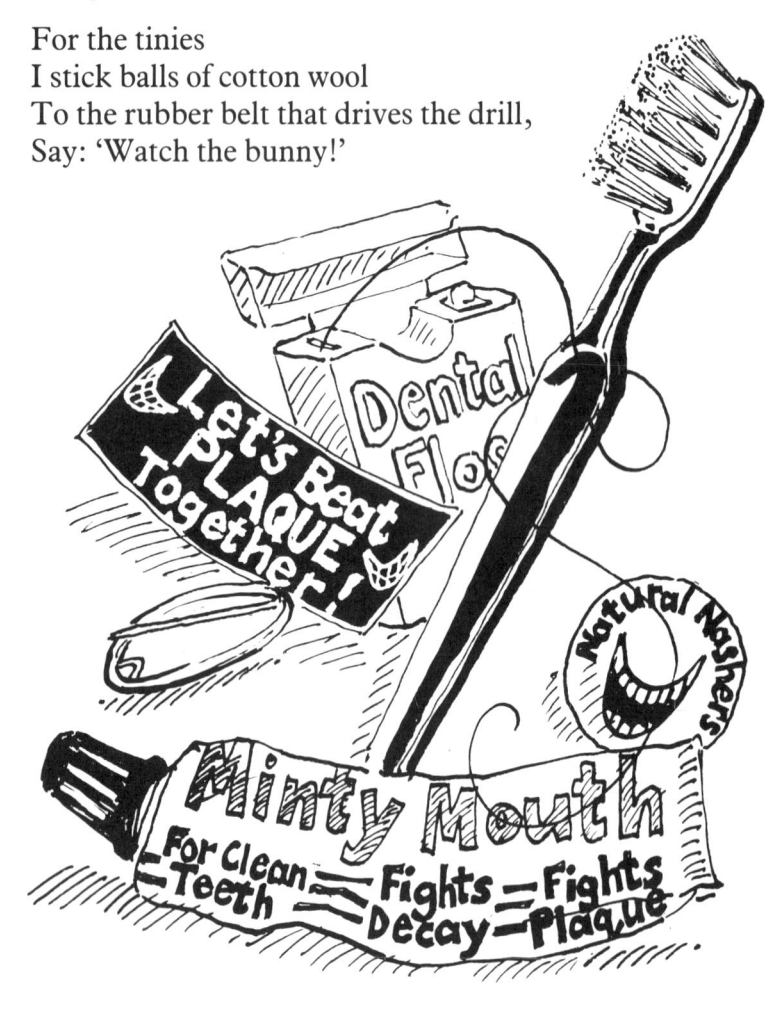

For the tinies
I stick balls of cotton wool
To the rubber belt that drives the drill,
Say: 'Watch the bunny!'

For the older ones the chair becomes
A spaceship: '5-4-3-2-1!'
I let them ride it up and down
For hours.

All that effort, all that time and trouble,
You'd think they'd like me,
Trust me just *a little*?
Not a hope.

All it takes is those few magic words:
'Now open wide . . .'
They start to scream and punch,
They kick. But why?

If I *wanted* to hurt their teeth
I'd be an ice-cream seller, run a sweet shop.
Would they hate me then? Oh, no!
I'd be their favourite person!

Best Friends

Sybil says:

If you don't let me ride the bike
    And push the doll's pram –

If you don't let me be the Mum
    And you be all the children –

If you don't let me be the queen
    And you be all the peasants –

If you don't let me swing
    And you do all the pushing –

Then I won't like you any more and
    I won't be your friend.

So I say:

. . . O K – and let her.

Because I couldn't
    Ride and push and swing,
    Be the Mummy and the queen
All on my own . . .
                    Could I?

Day Dreaming

Sometimes I close my eyes and let
the sounds flood in. Each
stair creak, distant radio,
the water chugging in the pipes,
my sister singing far below –
mix, blend and clash,
a mad band playing
just for me.

Sometimes I stop my ears and listen
to all the whisperings in my head
and everything I've ever heard or
known comes back. The fragments
whirl around – now here, now gone – like
tiny dust specks in a beam of light: I can't
explain. But what I see and hear and *know*
are things that only I know.

Sometimes I let myself drift
far away, and in a half-sleep world
I live in other places, other times
in other lives – short as a breath
or long as all of history.
I have been so many people, done
so many things – there isn't anything I couldn't do
(as long as I just stay here safe in bed . . .)

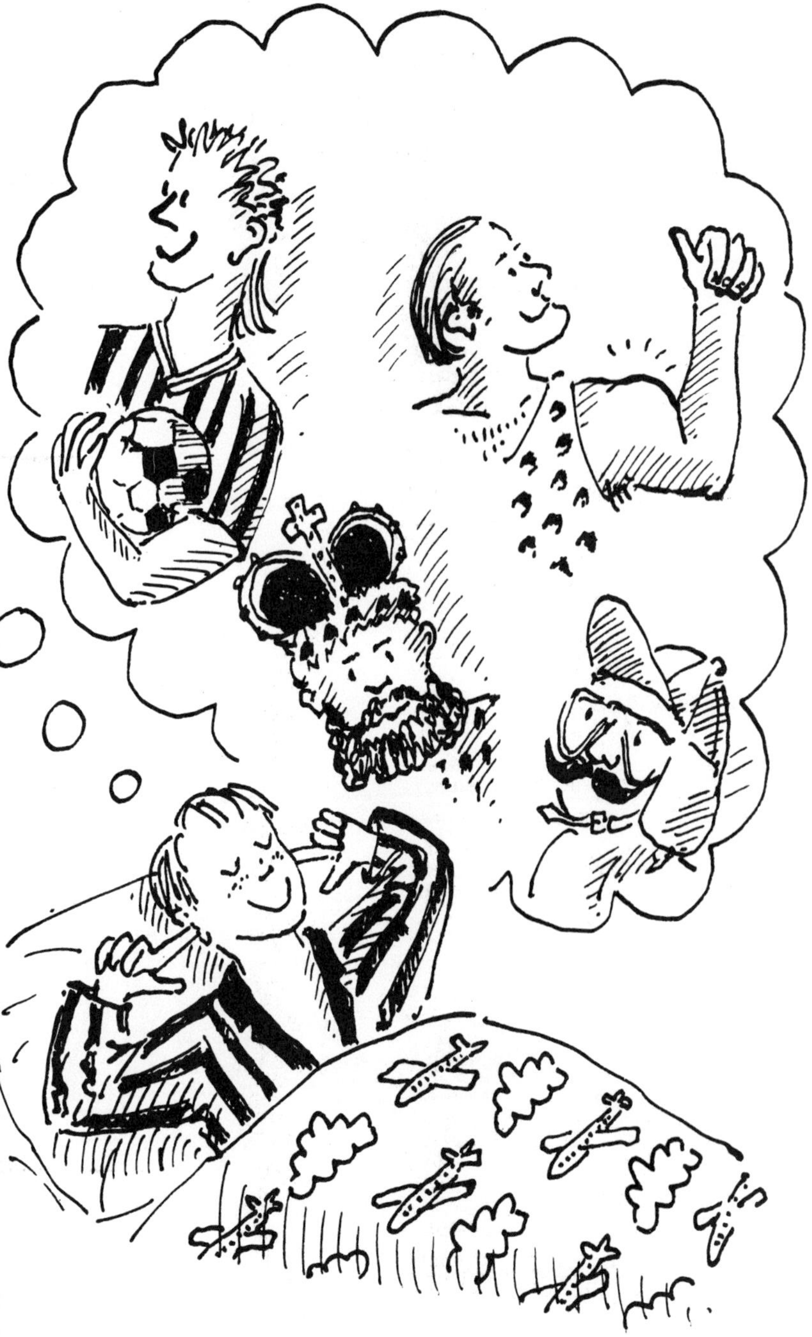

Building a Snowman

Building a snowman,
pressing muffled whispers
from the first fresh snow.

Further and fatter
two snowpips, sticky-wrapped, roll
snug in thick white pith.

He'll melt tomorrow
or the next day, but till then
– here's buttons, eyes, nose . . .

Done. His mouth beams back:
an old pipe in the corner,
a green twig grinning.

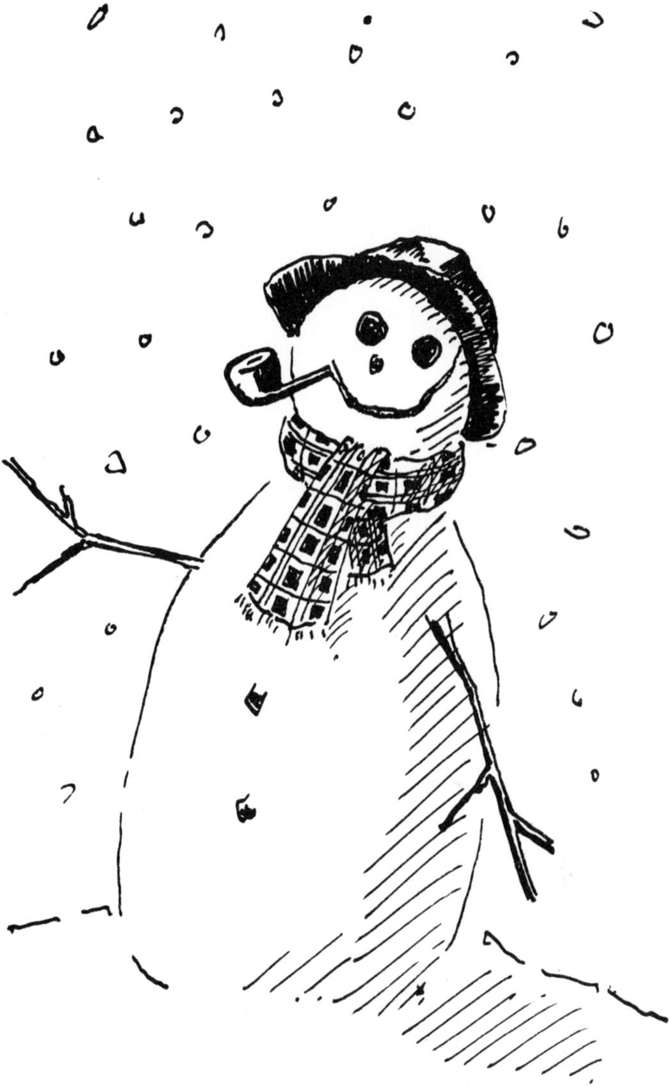

Scary Monsters

I love blood
I love gore
Horror movies – give me MORE.

I think Dracula's brilliant
And Frankenstein is a ball,
'Halloween 3'
Is my cup of tea,
'I Spit on your Chainsaw'
I'd queue in the rain for,
'The Unquiet Grave'
Is just what I crave
    And I never get frightened at all.
    No, I never get frightened at all.

I love blood
I love gore
Horror movies – give me MORE.

I adore all the bloodiest moments
Like the scenes when the heads start to fall,
My recreation
Is decapitation,
My lips begin smackin'
When vampires start snackin',
What gets me besotted's
The dripping carotids
    And I never get frightened at all.
    No, I never got frightened at all.

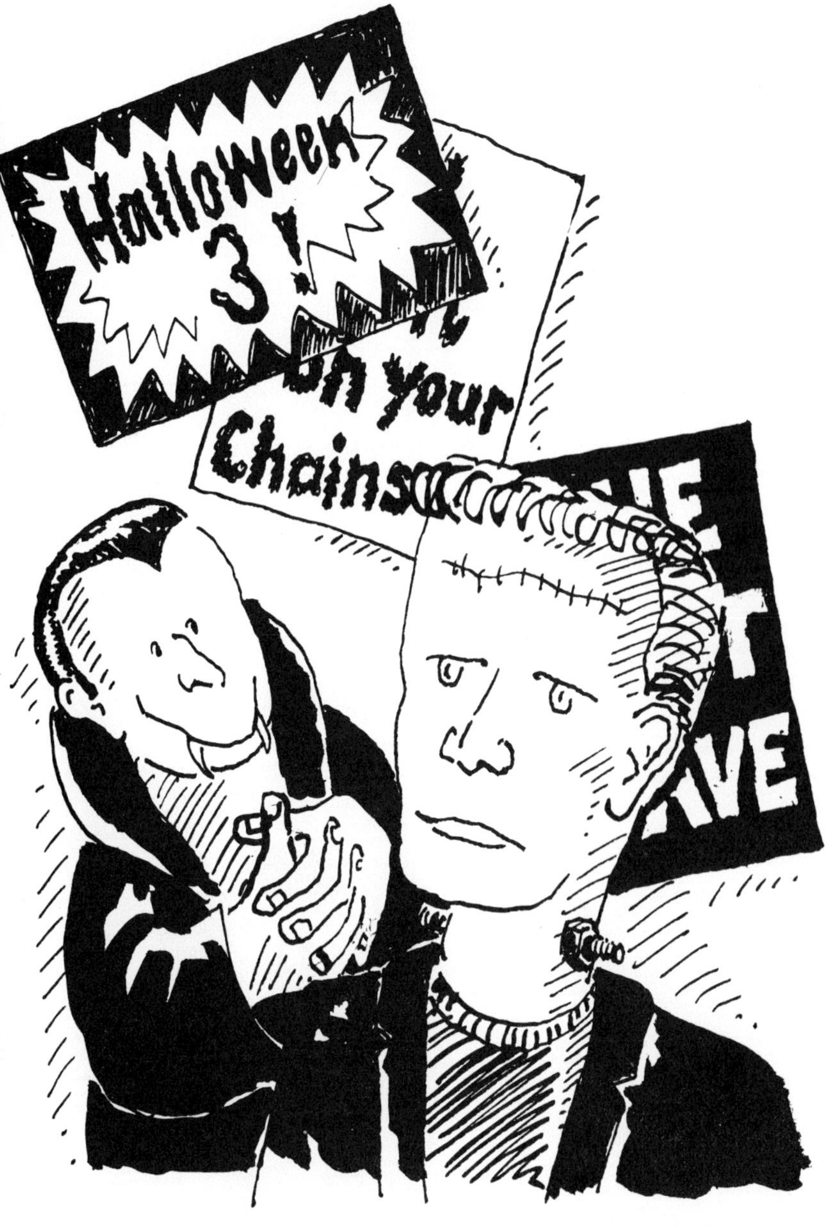
Halloween
3!
on your
Chains

I love blood
I love gore
Horror movies – give me MORE.

But . . . Late at night
When my room is black
And the Zombies prowl
With the Werewolf pack
And the Vampire dares
To climb the stairs

In the wee small hours of the night . . .

Then Mum stands guard on the landing
And Dad's at the foot of the stairs
While I sit on the loo with the radio on
And the door wide open
And sing my song:
        (*oh, i love blood,*
        yes, i love gore,
        horror movies – give me more.)

Shoplifting

'I dare you!'
   says a little voice
   soft and sly and very wicked.

'You can show them
   you ain't chicken
   you ain't yeller

– Are you? Are you?'

'I dare you!'
   says a little voice
   from deep inside.

'Show them all that
   you're a man
   you're tough and hard

– You can do it! You can do it!'

'I dare you!'
   says the little voice.
   'It's easy, anyone can do it

Show them what you're made of –
   – Quick! Now!
         Do it! Do it! Do it! Do it!'

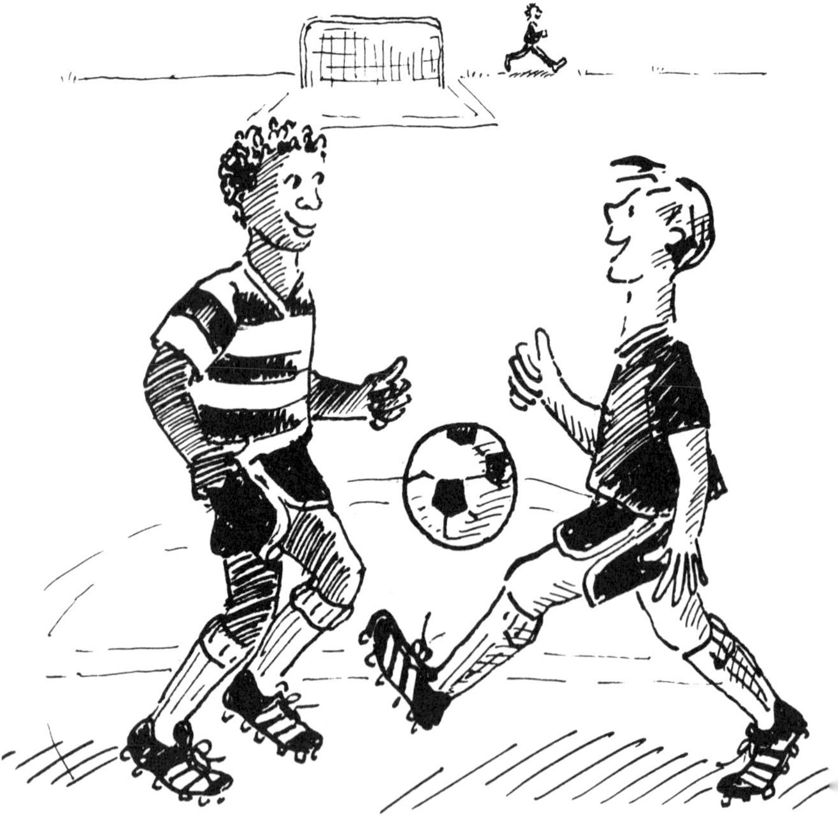

Boots

It's chilly on the touchline, but
with all my kit on
underneath my clothes
I'm not too cold. Besides,
I've got a job to do:
    I'm Third Reserve,
    I run the line.

I've been the Third Reserve all season,
every Saturday.
I've never missed a match.
At Home, Away:
it's all the same to me:
    'Cos I'm the Third Reserve,
    The bloke who runs the line.

That's my reward
for turning up
to every practice session, every
circuit training. Everything.
No one else does that –
    To be the Third Reserve,
    To run the line.

No chance of substitutions.
Broken ankles on the pitch
mean someone else's chance, not mine.
One down –
         and still two more to go:
  When you're the Third Reserve
  You run the line.

When I was first made Third Reserve
my Dad and me went out
and bought new boots. I keep them in the box.
I grease them every week
And put them back.
  When you're the Third Reserve –
  you know the score –
  You run the line in worn-out daps.

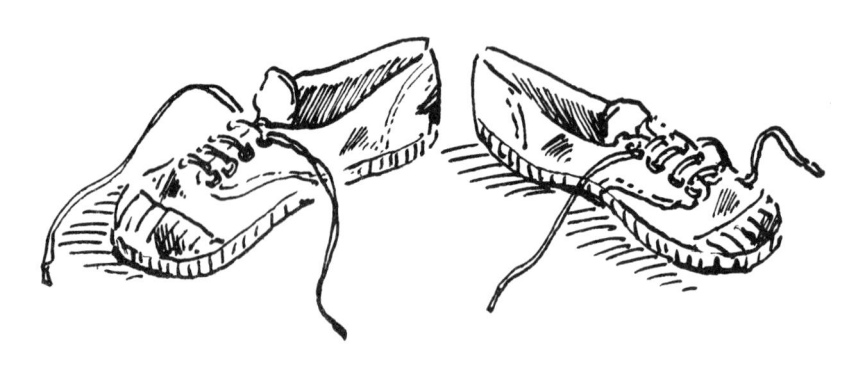

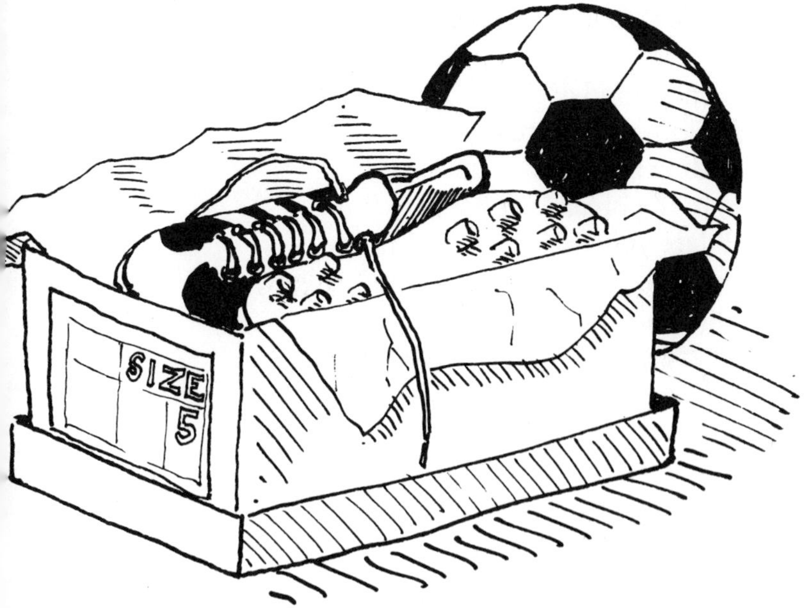
SIZE
5

Index of First Lines

A cholmond of mine	18
Building a snowman,	66
Hiding here	53
I am the breaker of bones	30
'I dare you!'	71
I give them 'Natural Nashers' badges,	60
I love blood	68
I started as an empty tortoise shell,	58
If I can get from here	8
If you come round to play with me	14
In Art we're always drawing cards	38
It's chilly on the touchline, but	73
My father was the mirror on the wall	44
My sister was only	40
On a normal, average day in our house:	32
Once upon a time there was a girl called Annabell.	20
Sally hasn't talked to me for ages.	10
Small black-and-white cat –	34
Some kids have fairies or friends you can't see	28
Some things are true	7
Sometimes I close my eyes and let	64
Sports Day's over.	46
Sybil says:	63
The teachers saw	50
Today is the first day of my new book.	56
What can kill a man	16

Answers to the Riddles

p. 16 *Machine Riddle 1*
       Computer
p. 30 *Machine Riddle 2*
       Car
p. 44 *Machine Riddle 3*
       Television
p. 58 *Machine Riddle 4*
       Guitar